THE BATTLE OF PASSCHENDAELE

Written by David Long

CONTENTS

BRITAIN AT WAR

On 4 August 1914, Britain declared war on Germany. More than a century after fighting began, **historians** are still arguing about the reasons behind a war which lasted for more than four years and killed around 17 million people. One significant battle was fought over a small village in Belgium called Passchendaele. Thousands of men died at Passchendaele, a place none of the soldiers had ever heard of before they joined the army.

Germany is often blamed for starting the First World War by **invading** Belgium. But the route to war started before this.

Years before war started, two powerful groups of **allies** had formed. On one side were Britain, France and Russia, known as the "Triple Entente". On the other side were the German Empire and Austria-Hungary, known as the "Central Powers".

Britain

Fra

Spain

Portugal

2

Norway

Sweden

Denmark

Netherlands

Belgium

The German
Empire

Switzerland

Russia

Austria-Hungary

Romania

Bosnia

Serbia
The Balkans

Italy

Bulgaria

Albania

Greece

Turkey

	Triple Entente
	Central Powers
	Neutral

3

King George V ruled the British Empire, which covered a quarter of the world including India, much of Africa, Canada, Australia and New Zealand. Kaiser Wilhelm II, who ruled Germany, wished to stop the British Empire growing even larger, and he also wanted an empire of his own by **acquiring** land in Africa. Britain didn't want Germany to become more powerful.

King George V

War fact

Tsar Nicholas II, Kaiser Wilhelm II and King George V were cousins.

Tsar Nicholas II

4

France, led by Prime Minister Raymond Poincaré, wanted to win back **territory** it had lost to Germany over 40 years before. Russia, ruled by **Tsar** Nicholas II, had clashed with the Germans over territory in the **Balkans**.

Raymond Poincaré

Kaiser Wilhelm II

Britain had the world's largest navy; France and Russia had large armies. They all wanted to hold on to their power and territory, and they felt threatened because Germany's navy was expanding.

5

On 28 June 1914, the heir to the throne of Austria-Hungary, Archduke Franz Ferdinand, was **assassinated** while he was on a visit to Sarajevo, Serbia. In response, on 28 July, Austria-Hungary supported by Germany, declared war on Serbia. Russia supported Serbia, and on 2 August, Germany then declared war on Russia. On 4 August, Germany declared war on Russia's ally, France.

the assassination of Archduke Franz Ferdinand

War is declared.

THE DAILY MIRROR, Wednesday, August 5, 1914.

GREAT BRITAIN DECLARES WAR ON GERMANY.

The Daily Mirror

LATEST CERTIFIED CIRCULATION MORE THAN 1,000,000 COPIES PER DAY

One Halfpenny.

No. 3,364.   Registered at the G.P.O. as a Newspaper.   WEDNESDAY, AUGUST 5, 1914.

DECLARATION OF WAR BY GREAT BRITAIN AFTER UNSATIS-
FACTORY REPLY TO YESTERDAY'S ULTIMATUM.

Neptune's imps. They are torpedo-boats steaming in close order to enable them to send verbal messages one to another by means of a megaphone.

6

Kaiser Wilhelm II's plan was to invade France and then Russia, and the quickest way to get to France was to march through Belgium. Britain had made an agreement with Belgium that it would protect that country.
When the Germans invaded Belgium, Britain declared war on Germany.

Soon after Britain had declared war, other countries joined in, on both sides, because their governments believed they could do well out of the war by becoming more powerful than their neighbouring countries.

German soldiers march through Belgium.

Joining up to fight

The news that Britain had declared war on Germany was welcomed by many ordinary British men and women.
With a sense of pride, **patriotism** and adventure, thousands of men rushed to join the army and navy. Most did this even though they'd no idea where Belgium was or why they should defend it.

Many welcomed the opportunity to fight for king and country. Army pay seemed generous to the poor and unemployed, and in a world where many went hungry so did the free food, called **rations**. Soldiers were paid one shilling a day, which is worth 5p today. They were also given free accommodation.

army recruitment posters encouraging young men to sign up

8

Army recruiting offices quickly appeared in towns all over the country. At first, the government wanted 100,000 volunteers, but in less than two months half a million men had applied to join the army and navy. Many joined what were called "Pals **battalions**" made up of friends, neighbours and colleagues from the same factories and offices. The war offered these men the excitement of going to another country at a time when many had never travelled far from where they were born.

However, even this number of recruits wasn't enough. With victory nowhere in sight and the number of **casualties** rising, the government was soon forced to introduce conscription. This meant fit young men had to leave their jobs and go and fight, even if they didn't want to.

By law, soldiers had to be over 18 years old to serve overseas, but approximately 250,000 boys lied about their age.

War fact

One boy called Sidney Lewis joined up when he was only 12.

THE WESTERN FRONT

Thousands of men were sent to fight on the Western Front – the name given to a **vast** area of land in France and Belgium. Most of the men were foot soldiers, known as infantry, but there were also cavalry soldiers, who rode into battle on horseback.

Many of the war's biggest battles took place on the Western Front, but the fighting turned into a stalemate. First one side would seem to be winning and then the other side – neither side was willing to surrender and neither seemed able to beat the other.

soldiers travelling by train on their way to the Western Front

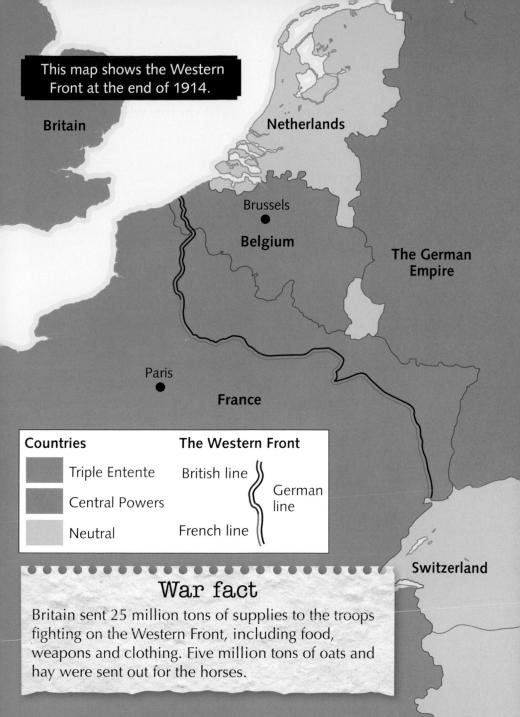

This map shows the Western Front at the end of 1914.

Britain

Netherlands

Brussels

Belgium

The German Empire

Paris

France

Countries

Triple Entente

Central Powers

Neutral

The Western Front

British line

German line

French line

Switzerland

War fact

Britain sent 25 million tons of supplies to the troops fighting on the Western Front, including food, weapons and clothing. Five million tons of oats and hay were sent out for the horses.

11

THE TRENCHES

When the British and the Germans realised that no side
was winning, they made preparations for a long war.
On the Western Front, this meant **excavating** long lines of
defensive trenches stretching more than 644 kilometres
from Switzerland to the North Sea. Now, rather than
marching or riding into battle, men on both sides sheltered
in their trenches, often for weeks at a time. This was now
a "trench war".

The idea of burrowing into the ground to avoid gunfire and
shellfire wasn't new: soldiers had been doing it 50 years
before the First World War began. It was a good **tactic**
to use. Once an enemy's dug-in, it becomes very difficult to
dislodge him. Soldiers must move forward to win battles,
but trenches prevent this happening. Before long, the war
had slowed almost to a halt.

LIFE IN THE TRENCHES

While the commanders were making plans and working out
how to break the stalemate, thousands of men on both sides
were stuck in the trenches. They lived there, day and night,
for weeks at a time. This network of long, deep ditches was
an uncomfortable place to be, even without the threat of
attack from a well-armed enemy.

In the winter, the ditches would fill with water which would sometimes freeze over. In warmer weather, they'd fill with flies, attracted by the smell of rotting bodies which were often left unburied because it was too dangerous for anyone to leave the trench to remove them.

Water filled the trenches.

Rats were also a big problem. Millions of them lived in the trenches, clambering over the men when they trying to sleep and feeding on the corpses until many were the size of cats. It was easy to kill individual rats, and soldiers often did, but the rats **bred** so fast that the numbers grew and grew. Nearly all the men suffered from **infestations** of lice as well – tiny, biting insects which hid in the soldiers' uniforms and sucked their blood.

Life for the men alternated between terror and boredom. If they weren't attacking the enemy trenches, or being attacked themselves, soldiers would have a dull daily routine. An hour before dawn, anyone who'd fallen asleep would be woken up and told to "stand to", meaning they had to get ready for an attack.

If the enemy didn't attack, breakfast would be carried from the service trenches behind the main trenches and eaten standing up. Afterwards, guns and weapons would be cleaned and inspected. The men also checked to see they weren't suffering from trench foot. This was an infection that was caused by standing in cold, wet water.

War fact

The average life expectancy for soldiers in the trenches was about six weeks.

Official rat-catchers used dogs to kill the rats in the trenches.

15

The men had a series of daily chores. Some would fill sandbags, which provided a bit of protection from shells and bullets. Others repaired the wooden duckboards the men walked on, or tried to pump out some of the water. Men also had to dig latrines – the name given to trench toilets – or maintain sections of the trench to ensure they were battle ready.

a soldier reading in the trenches

soldiers using a periscope
to spy on the enemy

An attack could come at any time, day or night, and so men
were posted along the length of each trench to keep an eye
on the enemy. It was vital that anyone doing this kept out of
sight to avoid being shot. Soldiers could do this by keeping
their head below ground level and looking over the top of
the trench with a periscope – a kind of telescope that can
see round corners or over a wall.

A Tommy's Kit

Although their meals were provided, British soldiers, called Tommies, were meant to be a self-contained fighting unit. This meant that each soldier had to carry everything he needed on his back.

The most important equipment was the weapons, which included a rifle and ammunition, a bayonet and some **grenades**. A gas mask was also essential, together with strong boots, a helmet, a cape or groundsheet to sleep on, and puttees. Puttees were long strips of cloth designed to be wound around both legs from knee to ankle, just above the boots. Unfortunately, they were little use in the damp, muddy conditions in which the soldiers lived.

War fact

At the start of the war, a soldier's daily ration included meat, bread and vegetables but the amount they were given was reduced as food became **scarce**.

18

helmet

cap

pouches
for
bullets

coat

bayonet

Puttees

boots

rifle

grenade

Soldiers were also issued with webbing equipment, the name
given to a type of thick, strong cotton material. A bag
made of this, called a haversack, contained personal items
such as cutlery for eating, shaving kit and a water bottle.
Most soldiers also had soap and a towel, although it
was impossible to wash or dry themselves properly in
the trenches. Each Tommy was given a trench tool –
a combined spade and pickaxe for digging trenches. This kit
could keep a soldier alive, but the battle ahead was bigger
than any they'd fought in before.

No Man's Land

The German trenches were a few hundred metres away from the British trenches. The area between the trenches was called "No Man's Land". This was a strip of land that didn't belong to either side. It was covered in **mines** and barbed wire. Soldiers crossing it to attack the enemy's trenches could be killed by an exploding mine, and they had nowhere to hide if they came under attack from enemy guns. Heavily-armed battalions of soldiers faced each other for month after month across the muddy, blasted landscape of No Man's Land. This is how millions of men spent much of the war, and it's where so many died.

War fact

No Man's Land was also the scene of a famous football match played during a brief **truce** on Christmas Day, 1914. Troops on both sides put down their weapons, and the Germans played football against the British. The Germans won the game 3–2.

21

PASSCHENDAELE

To break the stalemate of trench war, senior commanders on both sides spent their time studying maps and plans. They were trying to identify places along the front where they might break through the enemy's line. One of the places the British commanders believed this would be possible was Passchendaele – a small Belgian village in an area known as Flanders. It was surrounded by trenches and barbed wire and, by 1917, it'd been occupied by German troops for several years.

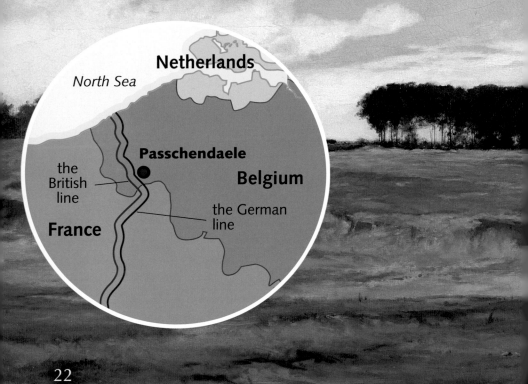

Netherlands

North Sea

Passchendaele

the British line

Belgium

the German line

France

The landscape of Flanders made it a very difficult place to fight. It was mostly very flat which made it more or less impossible to sneak up unseen on the enemy. The land would also have flooded without the series of man-made **dykes** and drainage ditches which crisscrossed the fields. Areas of raised ground were therefore potentially valuable, and many battles and **skirmishes** took place as each side attempted to take control of one dry ridge or another.

This painting shows what Passchendaele looked like before the fighting began.

For this reason, the British commander, Sir Douglas Haig, was determined to recapture Passchendaele. He thought success here would boost **morale** along the front and also back home where people had tired of the long war. A victory would also make it easier for Haig's troops to reach the Belgian coast. Once there, they could destroy the enemy submarines which were attacking British vessels in the English Channel and North Sea. Haig was also convinced that it would crush the German spirit, as he mistakenly believed that most German soldiers were too exhausted to fight on.

Sir Douglas Haig

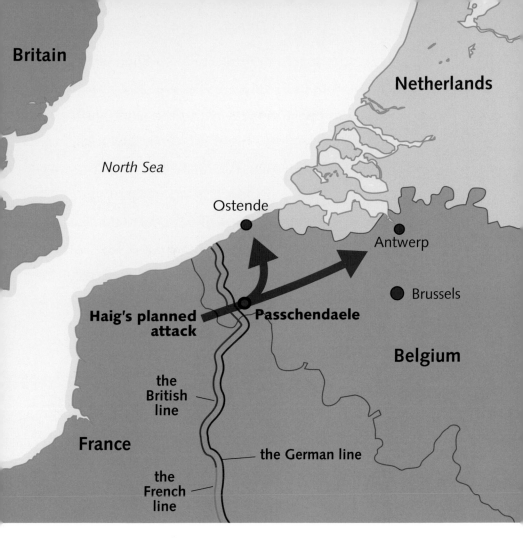

Haig wasn't alone in thinking in this way. Many military experts shared his view that this "race to the sea" was the key to winning the war. Although neither side was prepared to abandon its trenches, repeated attempts were made by the British and the Germans to defeat the other and gain control of the land running down to the coast.

In June 1917, British commanders in the region were at last able to report an important victory. This was in the Battle of Messines. For several weeks, 2,200 large and powerful field guns firing an incredible three million shells had pounded the German trenches. At the same time, the British were up to something else. Below ground, military miners called "sappers", had dug a series of 19 secret tunnels directly beneath the German lines. These were filled with around 400 tonnes of high explosive. When it was **detonated**, it was the largest man-made explosion ever recorded.

The noise from the explosion could be heard as far away as London, and a group of French scientists actually thought they were witnessing an earthquake. At Messines itself, the effects were devastating. Vast craters opened up, the largest nearly 80 metres in diameter, and more than 10,000 German soldiers simply vanished. It was the largest explosion anyone had ever witnessed.

The British troops assumed that any surviving Germans wouldn't be able to defend themselves, and they scrambled out of their trenches and launched the assault. German defenders were badly disorientated by the blast, but they fought back. They killed 3,538 British troops and wounded another 20,000, before finally accepting defeat. Victory meant the British now held the high ground of Messines Ridge and could get ready to sweep down on Passchendaele.

The explosives caused massive destruction to the German trenches.

131. MINE CRATER
MESSINES RIDGE.

THE BATTLE BEGINS

An incredible 3,000 big guns spent ten days firing
at the German trenches around Passchendaele.
After nearly 4.5 million shells had been fired, British and
French infantry then launched their first assault at dawn on
31 July 1917.

Storm clouds meant that it was still quite dark when the men
climbed out of their trenches. They attacked in a line more
than 16 kilometres long, and the men at one end quickly
achieved their objective. After pushing the enemy back
about 1.5 kilometres, more than 5,000 Germans
were taken prisoner. Unfortunately, faced
with heavy firing from the German lines,
the soldiers at the other end of the line
were less successful.

soldiers 'going over the top' –
climbing out of the trenches to
attack the enemy

heavy rain made fighting difficult

As the battle continued, torrential rain turned the whole area into a cold, black swamp. Within days, thick mud caused rifles to jam and meant many of the tanks couldn't move. Before long, the **quagmire** was so deep that men and horses were actually drowning in it, and there was a pause in the fighting.

Another assault was made in mid-August, but this too failed. After four days of ferocious fighting, British troops had hardly managed to move forward at all. Many more of them had been killed and wounded, but nothing had been achieved. For another month, there was stalemate and despite careful planning neither side seemed able to claim a **decisive** advantage.

In September, the weather improved and elsewhere on the Western Front, British troops scored some small but significant victories. By early October, they held an important ridge of high ground near the town of Ypres. A short spell of dry weather made it slightly easier to supply soldiers in the trenches with more ammunition. It also meant British and French aircraft could fly over the battlefield and spy on enemy positions down below.

British airmen planning their flight over the battlefield.

a German underground concrete
bunker used as a first-aid post

This succeeded in boosting the men's spirits. It may also
have helped encourage the belief that the German army's
morale was badly damaged and that it'd soon collapse.
Unfortunately, this turned out not to be true. Hiding in
strong, concrete bunkers, many Germans hadn't been
affected at all by the rain. This meant they were able to fight
back as fiercely as ever.

It was the British and French soldiers who were exhausted and becoming disheartened. German troops were now appearing on the battlefield in even greater numbers. Thousands of well-armed soldiers had come from the Eastern Front where they'd been fighting against Russia. Now, they succeeded in beating back the British.

War fact

The biggest gun of the war was a 48-tonne German howitzer. Nicknamed "Big Bertha" it could fire a shell nearly 19 kilometres.

a big gun being moved into position

Even the smallest attack or counterattack could lead to huge numbers of men being killed or injured. A pattern was soon established with one side successfully pushing forward before it was pushed back again by the opposing force. Every time this happened, there were hundreds of casualties.

Haig's hope for a "big push" all the way to the Belgian coast now looked like it would have to be abandoned. British commanders began to focus on smaller, more achievable goals instead. Now they hoped only to advance more slowly by taking smaller and smaller pieces of territory from German control.

German soldiers surrendering

MUD

The attack on Passchendaele had taken place across a vast area of low-lying land covered in a network of ditches and drainage channels. In peacetime, these were essential to prevent this rich farmland from flooding. Now, constant shelling from both sides had destroyed the drainage system and churned up the heavy clay soil.

Torrential rain, the worst for 30 years, made the situation even worse. In August 1917, twice as much rain fell as in an average year so that the clay was soon waterlogged. The following month was slightly better, but then in October more than 30 millimetres of rain fell in just five days, making an already difficult situation harder still.

All water naturally drains to the lowest point, which in the fields around Passchendaele meant it flooded into the trenches. The dust and flies of summer had now given way to thick, sticky mud which was even harder for the men to cope with. It clung to everything it touched. Soldiers' uniforms were soon caked in it. Guns jammed, and even tanks became bogged down and useless.

large tanks got stuck in the mud on the battlefield

In places, the gloopy mud was so deep that parts of the battlefield were now impassable. Lines of trenches had to be abandoned, and shell holes, which might have provided an alternative place to shelter, quickly filled with water. Already exhausted by the long war, men now had to fight their way through liquid mud and they frequently drowned. Those who survived faced a daily struggle just to get through the cold, stinking, waist-deep swamp.

Soldiers built walkways of wood over the mud.

High and dry. Some of the German positions weren't affected by the rain.

Only a few areas along the front were unaffected, including several enemy firing positions. For the Germans defending these positions, the rain must've seemed like a gift. Writing in his diary, one of the German officers described the dreadful weather as the "most fortunate rain, our most effective ally".

ARTILLERY BARRAGE

Before either side could launch an assault on the trenches of the other, the commanders would order an **artillery** barrage. This involved large field guns and howitzers, often many hundreds of them at a time. These heavy weapons would be wheeled into positions and would then fire millions of explosive shells at the enemy.

Such barrages formed a vital part of any attack, although they weren't always successful. Without the barrage, many of the soldiers leading the assault would've been shot within seconds of leaving their trenches. Any who escaped being hit would've found it almost impossible to reach safety through the mines and barbed wire of No Man's Land.

The barrages were intended to reduce the enemy's ability to fight back and to drive defenders out of their trenches. Shells fired into No Man's Land could also be used to explode enemy mines and to destroy the coils of barbed wire. This made it possible for attacking troops to leave their trenches and run towards the enemy. Otherwise they'd have to slowly pick their way through the wire which meant they were much more likely to be shot dead.

soldiers loading shells

The chief drawback of a barrage was that it warned the enemy that an attack was about to happen. However, the noise and danger

meant it could also be used to damage morale. By firing shells nonstop for several days and nights, it was possible to wear down the enemy still further by preventing the soldiers from getting even a few minutes' sleep.

Both sides used this tactic again and again. Sometimes the big guns could be arranged in a line that stretched for more than a kilometre. In this way, nearly a million shells could be fired in a single day.

big guns lined up to fire a barrage

GAS!

One of the most **sinister** weapons to be introduced during the war was poison gas. Its use had been **illegal** for several years before 1914, but French troops used gas-filled grenades within days of the war beginning. Soon soldiers on both sides were using gas to terrify, disable and kill.

an artist's impression of how gas affected soldiers

There were four different types used: tear gas, mustard gas, **chlorine** gas and **phosgene** gas. It was cheap to make, and gas quickly proved itself to be a **formidable** weapon. However, it was difficult to control the gas once it'd been released. If the wind changed direction, the gas would drift back towards the men who'd fired it. Despite this, the gas often found its target and the number of casualties in the trenches at Passchendaele began to climb.

Gas is heavier than air and it automatically sank down into the trenches. To begin with, soldiers tried to protect

themselves by wetting a handkerchief with urine, and then holding the handkerchief up to their face and breathing through the cloth. Eventually gas masks were issued to every soldier but these were heavy and uncomfortable. Some early models were also very difficult to put on in a hurry.

Different poisons had different effects. The tear gas in the French grenades was so weak that many German soldiers didn't realise they'd been attacked. Ghostly green clouds of chlorine were deadlier. The gas reacted with moisture in the soldiers' lungs to produce **hydrochloric acid**. It caused such pain and damage to a soldier's body that breathing it in could easily kill a man.

Even dogs wore specially made gas masks in the trenches.

Mustard gas got its name from its sickly yellow colour and the smell. It caused painful blisters on the skin and in the lungs, which made it impossible for

War fact

90,000 soldiers were killed by gas.
185,000 soldiers were injured by gas.

soldiers to continue fighting. Mustard gas also got trapped in the soil and remained poisonous. Phosgene gas is colourless and took a day or more to kill anyone who came in contact with it. As it was invisible, it had a devastating effect on morale. All it took was for one soldier to cough for everyone around him to think they were under attack.

soldiers with eye injuries caused by the effects of gas

43

NEW TECHNOLOGY

One of the most important ways in which the First World War was different from previous conflicts was in the widespread use of new technology.

With so many men fighting, battles were taking place in many different places around the world. Away from the fighting, inventors and scientists on both sides were racing to find new and deadlier ways to defend their own troops and to defeat the enemy. Soldiers still carried rifles and bayonets, but on the ground, in the air and at sea, new types of machine dramatically altered the way modern war was fought and won.

German soldiers with their new invention – a portable searchlight

This is one of the first British tanks. It was used in combat in 1916.

Britain produced the first armoured "landship" or tank in 1915. It was **cumbersome** and slow but proved so useful that similar devices were soon being developed in France and Germany. The quality of weapons also improved at an incredible rate. Early machine guns had been as heavy as cannon and took at least six men to operate, but now new versions began to appear. These were easier to handle and, firing more than ten rounds a second, they could produce a devastating hail of death when dozens were lined up together.

War fact

During one battle, the British fired their rifles so quickly – averaging 30 rounds per minute – that the Germans mistook them for machine guns.

New, lighter weapons could also be fitted to tanks and to aircraft. So far, aeroplanes had been used only to spy on the enemy from above or occasionally to drop small bombs. Now pilots could engage in dogfights, supporting troops down in the trenches at Passchendaele and along the front line, and defending them from enemy attack. The British also invented new glow-in-the-dark ammunition. Called tracer bullets, these emitted tiny amounts of a **flammable** chemical so that a soldier firing at night could see where he was aiming.

Britain's most successful pilot was Major Mick Mannock who shot down sixty-one enemy aircraft.

Royal Aircraft Factory SE 5A, the machine flown by Mannock

The Germans had their own flying hero. Manfred von Richthofen, known as the Red Baron, shot down eighty British and French aircraft.

Aircraft were also used at sea for the first time. Taking off from the world's first aircraft carriers – ordinary ships fitted with long, flat platforms – the aircraft could spot and attack submarines. A special kind of underwater bomb (a "depth charge") was designed to explode close to an enemy submarine, sending it to the bottom of the sea.

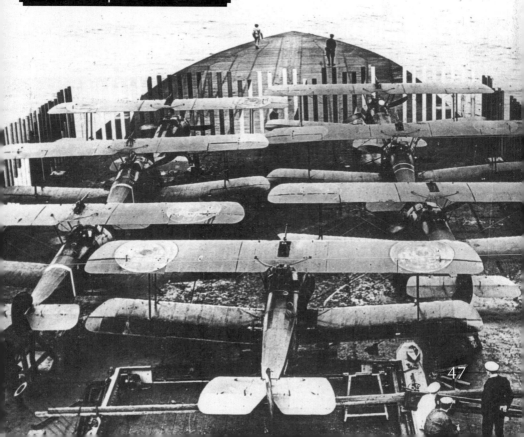

British aircraft carrier *Furious*, with aeroplanes on deck

ANIMALS AT WAR

Problems weren't always solved with new technology. Besides the hated rats and lice, soldiers in the trenches at Passchendaele were joined by animals that would help them win the war.

Machines like tanks were being used, but both sides started the war with large cavalry forces. Many soldiers still rode horses on the Western Front and camels in the desert campaigns of the Middle East. Even greater numbers of horses, together with donkeys and mules, were kept busy carrying ammunition, food and medical supplies to the front. The strongest ones were used for hauling heavy guns through the stinking mud.

the mud was so deep in some places the horses got stuck in it

Today we take telephones for granted, but armies in the First World War had to rely on animals to carry many of their messages from one place to another. Specially trained dogs could run faster and further than any of the men. They were also much harder for enemy **snipers** to shoot which meant supplies of ammunition and important information could be safely sent around the network of trenches.

War fact

More than 16 million animals served in the First World War.

Army pigeons were faster still. They **navigated** over huge distances and they could find their way back home. For such small animals, they also have incredible **stamina**; during the war, hundreds of pigeons successfully carried coded messages all the way back to England from the battle lines. The Germans knew what was going on, and often tried to shoot the pigeons. They hoped to be able to **decipher** the messages before cooking and eating the unfortunate bird.

Back in the trenches, canaries in cages were very good at detecting poisonous gas. If there wasn't an official rat-catcher with his dog, cats were used to hunt and kill the giant rats. Animals like this also provided comfort and companionship for the men.

pigeons carrying messages

This is a war memorial in London, which commemorates the bravery of animals in wartime.

Several animals also showed exceptional courage, saving lives in circumstances they must have found terrifying. A donkey named Murphy carried many wounded soldiers out of danger, and a pigeon called Cher Ami made a daring flight through enemy gunfire which led to the rescue of more than 200 men. Some animals even won medals for their work in the First World War, like Sergeant Stubby. Stubby was an American army dog, and he wore a coat with all his medals attached to it.

Sergeant Stubby

PASSCHENDAELE'S WAR OF ATTRITION

Even with all these new inventions, and the success of using animals, at Passchendaele both sides realised that the war would be won by the side with the most men and weapons. By attacking again and again, the enemy would eventually surrender when it had lost too many men to keep fighting. This is called a "war of attrition" (when an enemy is worn down to the point of collapse).

the French city of Verdun, which was destroyed by German troops

This tactic is controversial because it can prove extremely costly in terms of both lives and equipment. However, it's possible that commanders on both sides in the First World War felt they'd no alternative. They couldn't use conventional tactics such as ambushing the enemy or surrounding them so they had to prepare themselves for a long and deadly war.

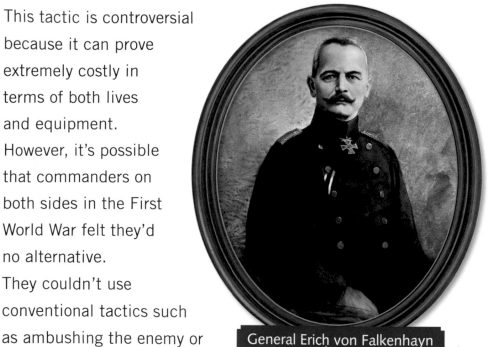

General Erich von Falkenhayn

General Erich von Falkenhayn, who commanded the German troops, admitted that his plan was not to overrun the enemy-held towns, but to destroy the troops defending them. He said he wanted to "bleed France white" – to kill every single enemy soldier. The senior commanders and politicians on both sides were willing to sacrifice thousands of their troops – at Passchendaele the life of the average soldier wasn't considered important.

EMPIRE TROOPS

One of the reasons the war became known as a world war was because it involved soldiers, sailors and airmen from almost every corner of the globe. This was partly because Britain had such a large empire. When Britain declared war on Germany, it meant the whole of the British Empire was at war. Just as men and women back home in Britain queued up to "do their bit" in 1914, so people in India, South Africa, Australia, Canada and New Zealand saw it as their duty to join the fight, too.

a poster encouraging men from the British Empire to join up and fight

The number of different nationalities who joined up to fight was huge, which is why it's a mistake to think that most of the fighting took place between the British, French and Germans. As many as four million Asians and Africans took part in the war, although they're rarely seen in photographs of life on the Western Front. At least a quarter of those who gave their lives fighting for Britain weren't British.

More than one and a half million men came from India, to defend a country they'd never seen. They served in Belgium and France but also fought in Italy, the Middle East and in West and East Africa. On the Western Front, four Indian soldiers were awarded the Victoria Cross, Britain's highest award for gallantry.

troops from India

In just two months, 32,000 Canadians signed up to fight. By the end of the war, they'd been joined by more than half a million of their countrymen.

The situation in Australia was similar. When the prime minister promised that his country would fight "to our last man and our last shilling", a total of 380,000 men enlisted. New Zealand, despite having a population of little more than a million, contributed an incredible 100,000 men.

Australian machine gunners

Mostly these were people who hadn't even visited Britain,
and in many cases they never would. Not everyone in
their own countries agreed with their decision to enlist.
but without them Britain might have lost the war.

War fact

More than half the Australians who
enlisted were killed or injured.

WRITING HOME

Letters to and from home were so important to the soldiers that the British army ran its own postal service. During the course of the war, two billion letters were sent and received this way, and at one point, nearly 20,000 bags of mail were crossing the English Channel every day.

Despite their difficult living conditions, soldiers like those at Passchendaele were usually able to find the odd moment in which to write a letter to their loved ones. Sometimes this was done from trenches on the front line, but there were rules **forbidding** anyone from writing down certain things. Letters were officially **censored** to ensure nothing was said which might help the enemy or make it sound like the war was going badly.

Even so, the men usually found ways to write what they wanted to say without being caught breaking the rules. This means their letters, many thousands of which are now **preserved** in museums, often provide fascinating personal insights into life in the trenches. Sometimes funny as well as touching and desperately sad, they can help us understand the experience of fighting in such a dreadful war.

a soldier writing home

PASSCHENDAELE – INCHING TOWARDS VICTORY

By the second week of October 1917, many of the British big guns located in the countryside around Passchendaele were out of action due to the rain and mud. Others had been wrecked by German artillery fire. Many more were too far from the front line, and moving them forward through the quagmire now looked impossible.

Refusing to give up, British troops sometimes managed to advance a few metres towards the village in the morning, but usually they were beaten back in the afternoon by enemy counterattacks. Together with the dreadful conditions on the battlefield, possibly the worst of the entire war, this demoralising process drained both the strength and spirit of the men.

many British soldiers like this man were exhausted by the battle

Fresh arrivals of soldiers from the Eastern Front also meant they were facing an even larger German force than before. In response, British army commanders called for reinforcements of their own, made up of Australians and New Zealanders – known as Anzacs – and later Canadians.

Casualties continued to rise on all sides. At one point in the fighting, Germany was losing a thousand men a day. On 12 October, more New Zealanders were killed or wounded than on any day in the country's entire history. The following morning Britain decided again to halt the **offensive** until the weather improved. This gave them a chance to repair trenches and rebuild several kilometres of roads, rails and tracks needed to move more big guns into better positions.

engineers working on a rail track

Special platforms where guns were fired from (gun emplacements) were also improved. When the fighting restarted two weeks later, the occupation of a few patches of higher ground gave Britain and her allies a slight advantage. Being able to see what was going on made it easier for officers to direct the battle. These higher, drier positions would also be useful if the campaign continued into the winter months.

guns were hidden under camouflage nets so enemy aircraft couldn't see them

Supported by British and French troops on one side and Anzacs on the other, the Canadians went into battle early in the morning of 26 October. They launched the assault in yet more heavy rain, and for more than a week, four divisions or groups of Canadians took turns attacking the Passchendaele ridge. The mud and rain steadily worsened, and sometimes a waterlogged shell crater was the only place anyone could find shelter.

The Canadians' first objective was to capture a ridge of high ground held by the Germans and, despite heavy losses, it looked like they were now poised to achieve this. A temporary improvement in the weather made it possible to resupply them with more weapons and ammunition. Four days later, following another extended period of heavy shelling of German positions, they renewed their attack. This time they reached the outskirts of Passchendaele and looked set, at last, to seize the village.

Before the battle, a Canadian commander had argued against it, fearing that as many as 16,000 of his men would be killed or wounded. In the event, his forecast turned out to be horribly accurate: by the time their comrades reached Passchendaele, 15,654 Canadian soldiers had been killed.

WHAT HAPPENED TO THE WOUNDED?

As well as 17 million dead, the war left more than 20 million people with terrible injuries.

The lucky ones were sent back home to be treated. In Britain, schools, universities, army camps and country houses were converted into large military hospitals. But more often men had to be treated on the battlefield in conditions which were uncomfortable and far more dangerous.

wounded soldiers being treated at Queen Mary's Hospital, Roehampton, London, 1918

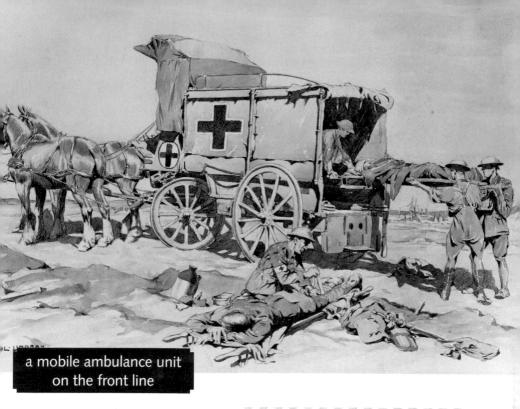

a mobile ambulance unit
on the front line

In the trenches like those at Passchendaele, men who were only slightly injured were given treatment wherever they were standing before being ordered to carry

on fighting. If their wounds were more serious, they'd be lifted out of the trenches on a stretcher. Once the fighting had quietened down, these men would be taken by motorised or horse-drawn ambulance to a temporary medical post behind the lines.

The most common injuries for those listed as wounded were to arms and legs, either from gunfire, barbed wire or nearby explosions. Head and body injuries accounted for a much smaller proportion but this might be because the men usually died before they could be treated.

There was also a very high risk of infection among men who were physically exhausted and living in filthy, muddy conditions. Many patients suffered the appalling effects of poisonous gas or trench foot. This could cause skin to rot and die.

Some soldiers were so badly injured they couldn't be helped. With little chance of survival, every attempt was made to make them comfortable but they received no medical treatment. Instead, priority had to be given to soldiers who were more likely to live.

injured soldiers in the trenches

a mobile X-ray unit

Medical care improved a lot as the war went on, with new advances such as blood transfusions and splints for broken bones. In 1914, four out of five men with a broken thigh died but by the end of the war just one out of five men died from the same kind of injury.

Other medical advances included Cellucotton, made from sugar cane, which made better, more absorbent bandages than traditional strips of fabric. The war also saw the first mobile X-ray machines, a French invention which helped improve the treatment of injured soldiers. Once the war was over, new **civilian** uses were found for these and other military inventions.

PASSCHENDAELE – THE BATTLE IS OVER

Following another massive artillery bombardment from British guns, and fierce and prolonged hand-to-hand fighting, Canadian troops finally overran soldiers defending the village and took them prisoner. What the soldiers later called the "Battle of Mud" was over at last.

Reaching the village had taken more than three months of tough combat. Yet during that time, Britain and her allies had managed to advance only eight kilometres across the devastated Flanders landscape. Now, having reached Passchendaele, the attackers found that there was almost nothing left of the village itself.

soldiers leaving the trenches

German prisoners of war

With such huge numbers of casualties on both sides, it was hardly the decisive victory everyone had hoped for. There was little or no celebrating. Instead, especially amongst those who survived the onslaught, the battle rapidly gained a reputation as one of the most terrible periods in the entire war.

For another four days, fighting continued further north in a bid to capture another area of high ground to the north of the village, but after this there were no more large-scale battles in this part of the Western Front. The war rumbled on but the focus moved away from Belgium and France.

AFTERMATH

Having captured Passchendaele, Haig almost immediately abandoned his plan to fight his way to the coast. Troops were diverted to Italy to stop the Austrian army's advance, and nearly a century later historians are still arguing about whether or not the Battle of Passchendaele was even worth fighting.

The casualties were amongst the worst of the war; it's estimated that more than 800,000 were killed, injured or missing. Tens of thousands of bodies have never been found, and many people still think the human cost was too high just to capture the ruins of a small Belgian village.

However, the battle marked an important turning point in the war. The months of fighting are now seen as the beginning of the end for Germany and her allies.

Soon afterwards, Russia pulled out of the war, but America had joined the war. By supporting Britain and France with fresh supplies of men and machinery, this did much to ensure Germany's eventual defeat.

In the years after the war, Haig was blamed for the huge number of lives lost and widely criticised for stubbornly sticking to his war plan even when it looked like the attack was unlikely to succeed. However, no one could've foreseen such awful weather nor fully grasped the dreadful impact of the resulting sea of mud. By deciding to fight a war of attrition, Haig was also counting on the high death rate affecting Germany's chances of success more than Britain's – which in the end it did.

After so long, the Battle of Passchendaele isn't seen in terms of success or failure, victory or defeat. For most it's seen as a tragic reminder of the real horror of war. Above all, it's come to symbolise the senseless slaughter that destroyed so many lives a hundred years ago.

PASSCHENDAELE TODAY

Months of heavy shelling meant that by the end of
the battle there was almost nothing left of Passchendaele.
In photographs taken by British pilots flying overhead, not
a single house could be seen standing. The village church
was completely ruined, roads show up only faintly against
the acres and acres of churned-up mud. Passchendaele was
all but wiped from the map.

But despite its near-total **obliteration**, it's still possible to
visit Passchendaele today and discover more about the battle
and the men who fought there. The church has been rebuilt
and contains several memorial windows to the dead. There's
also a museum which tells their story, and in the countryside
around the village are haunting **relics** of the war, including
a preserved section of trench.

aerial photographs of Passchendaele before and after the battle

Tyne Cot is the largest military cemetery in Europe. It's one of dozens scattered along the frontier between Belgium and France, beautifully maintained by the Commonwealth War Graves Commission, the organisation which looks after military cemeteries at battlefield sites around the world.

Tyne Cot contains almost 12,000 graves. The names of another 34,000 soldiers are carved into the long stone wall which surrounds the cemetery. These are men who were listed as missing but whose bodies have never been found after one of the worst battles in history.

GLOSSARY

acquiring   getting to own (something)

allies   countries which agree to fight on the same side

artillery   big guns used to destroy enemy trenches before an attack by troops

assassinated   killed (usually someone important or famous)

Balkans   an area which included Romania, Bulgaria, Croatia, and parts of Greece and Turkey in 1914

battalions   an organised body of several hundred soldiers

bred   produced babies

casualties   soldiers killed, wounded or missing after a battle

censored   removed information from soldiers' letters to make sure they weren't giving away military secrets

chlorine   a strong-smelling, greenish-yellow gas

civilian   a person who isn't in the army or navy

cumbersome   difficult to use or operate because of its large size or weight

decipher   work out the meaning of a secret code

decisive   able to make a choice quickly

detonated   when a bomb or mine explodes

dislodge   forcing an enemy soldier to come out from his hiding place

dykes   ditches used for draining water from farmland

excavating   digging a hole or trench

flammable   can be set on fire

forbidding   giving orders not to do something

formidable   strong or powerful, difficult to defeat

grenades   small but powerful bombs which are thrown by hand

historians   people who study the past

hydrochloric acid a dangerous liquid poison which can burn skin

illegal something which is forbidden by law

infestations overrun with pests, like rats

invading a country or group of people attempting to capture land belonging to another country

mines explosives hidden underground to kill or injure troops

morale the mood of a person or group of people

navigated found the route

obliteration destruction

offensive attack against enemy soldiers

patriotism the good feelings a person has about his or her country

phosgene a colourless, poisonous gas that smells like new-mown hay

preserved rescued and prevented from decaying or wearing out

quagmire a bog or marshy area of ground

rations a soldier's daily allowances of food and drink

relics historical survivors or souvenirs

scarce rare

skirmishes fights between small groups of soldiers

sinister evil and threatening

snipers soldiers who shoot at enemies from a hidden position

stamina strength and energy that keeps someone going for a long time

tactic a plan to achieve a goal

territory an area of land

truce an agreement to stop fighting for a short time

Tsar the ruler of Russia

vast very large

INDEX

LIFE ON THE WESTERN FRONT

No Man's Land

the trenches

rats

gas

mud

into battle

in the air

delivering messages

wounded in battle

writing home

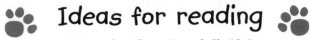

Ideas for reading

Written by Clare Dowdall, PhD
Lecturer and Primary Literacy Consultant

Reading objectives:
- discuss their understanding
- explore the meaning of words in context
- draw inferences and justify these with evidence

Spoken language objectives:
- ask relevant questions to extend understanding and knowledge
- participate in discussions, presentations, performances, role play, improvisations and debates

Curriculum Links: History – British History

Resources: ICT, papers and pens

Build a context for reading

- Ask children to share what they know about the First World War.
- Look at the front cover. Compare the scene with the children's ideas. Discuss the awful conditions and what life must have been like for soldiers. Notice the poppy and make connections to Poppy (Remembrance) day.
- Read the blurb together. Help children to pronounce the place name *Passchendaele* and check that children know that Belgium is in Europe.

Understand and apply reading strategies

- Read pp2–5 to the children. Locate Belgium on the map. Check and develop comprehension by asking them to recount who was involved (countries and individuals), referring to the illustrations and text for support.
- Discuss the emboldened words: *historians, invading, allies, territory, Balkans.* Ask children to suggest definitions explaining their reasons (context, root words). Use the glossary to check and find precise definitions.